THE GREAT BOOK OF

MOVIES F/X

THE GREAT BOOK OF

MOVIES F/X

Text by Ian Rimmer

Rourke Enterprises, Inc.
Vero Beach, FL 32964

Library of Congress Cataloging-in-Publication Data

Rimmer, Ian, 1955—
    Movies F/X.

    (The Great book of—)
    Includes index.
    Summary: Describes how various types of special effects are created in
films.
    1. Cinematography—Special effects—Juvenile literature.
[1. Cinematography—Special effects]
I. Title. II. Series.
TR858.R56   1988   778.5'345   87-36971
ISBN 0-86592-453-8

Contents

Seeing and Believing

Just as you shouldn't believe all you read in the papers, you shouldn't believe all you see in the movie theater. Much of what we think we see at the movies is actually brilliant illusion created by special effects artists. Their work is essential to movies. Throughout the years, movie makers have wanted to film scenes that aren't safe to shoot, aren't economical to shoot, or aren't even possible to shoot. When the story to be told demands such dangerous, expensive, or impossible scenes, it is the special effects designers who provide the audience with the visual images required.

Planet of the Apes — "make-up" effects.

PA-121-39

How Effects are Possible

Movies are, of course, a series of still pictures, or *frames*, projected in rapid succession. We see 24 frames every second when watching a film, and that gives us the impression that we are seeing continuous movement. It also gives the effects artist three opportunities to go to work.

First, although film is projected continuously, it doesn't have to be photographed continuously. Film can be exposed one frame at a time, so the subject being filmed can be altered in some way between frames. This is *stop-motion* photography.

Second, models, paintings, make-up, and anything else can be photographed in such a way that they look real. This *film illusion* includes the use of stunt people who double for actors while difficult or dangerous scenes are filmed.

Finally, different subjects that have been filmed separately can be combined to appear as though they were originally recorded together at the same time. Instead of seeing a single photograph in each frame, we're seeing a final *composite image* of two or more separate images.

These three "areas of intervention" enabled the earliest effects artists to astound their audiences. Even though modern day technology has given rise to electronic gadgetry and computer cameras, these techniques are still at the very heart of effects work today. Just about any special effects you've ever seen were produced using one or more of these areas of intervention.

1. Background scene filmed.

2. Model of bird filmed against a special blue background screen.

3. An opaque bird-shaped mask is made on clear film from the silouette of the bird.

4. The mask is printed against the background to create a "hole".

5. A mask with a bird-shaped hole is made for the final printing stage.

6. The bird is printed through the hole onto the bird-shaped area of unexposed background.

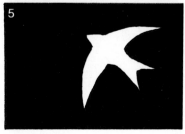

The Earliest Effects

Audiences had been watching magic lantern shows – single images projected on a screen – for many years. It was not until the end of the last century, though, that it was realized that photographs could be projected in quick succession if they were first taken on a continuous strip of celluloid film. And following the first public showing of "moving pictures" by the Lumière brothers of Paris, in 1885, music halls quickly embraced the new entertainment. Several illusionists incorporated moving pictures into their acts, and one, Georges Méliès, discovered that the new medium had enormous potential for "magic."

Stop Motion by Accident

Méliès had been photographing the streets of Paris when the film in his camera jammed for a short period. When he later projected this film, he saw that a carriage he had been focusing upon had suddenly become a hearse due to the gap in time when the film jammed.

Méliès then began stopping the film in his camera deliberately to make changes to a scene he was filming, and soon his L'Escomptage d'une Dame ("The Vanishing Lady," 1896) was thrilling audiences. It depicted a woman sitting in a chair and then vanishing. A skeleton then appears on the seat and disappears shortly thereafter to be replaced by the woman again. All these tricks were the first ever stop-motion special effects.

Muybridge — galloping horse 1878. Readers of Scientific American were invited to paste the pictures below on strips and view through a zoetrope — a precursor of motion pictures — a topless drum with slits in its side mounted on a spindle.

More Magic From Méliès

The Frenchman went on to discover that he could "save" areas of film by not exposing them. He would photograph himself in one area of the film, ensuring that the rest of it remained unexposed. Then he would carefully rewind the film, position himself in an area he had previously left unexposed, and begin filming again. When this composite image film was finally projected, Méliès appeared in many places, all seemingly at once.

With his theatre background, Méliès was well aware of what could be accomplished with scenery and make-up. This was evident in his most celebrated film, *La Voyage dans la Lune* ("Voyage to the Moon," 1902). In this film a professor, Méliès, fires a rocket to the moon; the rocket ends up stuck in the moon's eye. This scene is an example of film illusion, since the rocket was a model, and the moon was a heavily made-up actor with cleverly painted space scenery around his face. This 20-minute film, which used all of Méliès's illusions, could be described as the world's first science fiction epic. The age of the special effects movie had arrived.

Decades of Development

In the years that followed, effects grew in sophistication as cinema technology advanced. The advent of sound, and later of color, brought new challenges for effects designers. Yet for much of the time between the 1920s and 1950s, they found themselves working on incredible beasts and monsters. We'll look at some of that work in later chapters.

Metropolis (1926) City skyline.

There were several notable achievements by effects designers during these years. Among them was Fritz Lange's *Metropolis* (1926) which, thanks to Lange's earlier architectural training, featured some fantastic modeled city skylines and machinery from a metropolis of 2000 A.D. Another milestone was *The Invisible Man* (1933), which had at its core some superb "invisibility" set pieces created by John Fulton. Most chilling of these is the scene where the mad doctor, who has made himself invisible, peels away some bandages from his head – to reveal nothing underneath!

Fulton went on to create one of the film industry's greatest effects. He brought to the screen the Old Testament miracle of the parting of the Red Sea in Cecil B. De Mille's *The Ten Commandments*. This marvelous effect took 18 months to complete and cost an estimated one million dollars. It involved real footage of the Red Sea, painstakingly matched to torrents of water poured from huge dump tanks that flooded together in a vast studio set. The footage from the matched Red Sea and tank water was reversed, and this clever ploy worked perfectly to make the Red Sea appear to part. Then, of course, film of Moses and the Chosen People had to be added, along with the threatening storm clouds in the sky. This example of meticulous composite image work deservedly won Fulton the 1956 Oscar for Special Effects.

The Optical Printer

During this period, an indispensable machine for the effects artist was invented. The optical printer was developed by Linwood Dunn, along with Cecil Love and the Acme Tool Manufacturing Company. It made the combining and integrating of almost any separately filmed sequences possible. Basically, the original film is run through a projector and re-photographed by a movie camera, allowing extensive opportunities for effects.

For example, a mask can be inserted to keep an area of the repeat film unexposed. New filmed elements can then be added in the unexposed area. So, we might see someone looking in a mirror, but after re-filming in which the mirror reflection has been masked out, we'd be able to insert something other than his reflection in the mirror.

Additionally, an optical printer can enlarge elements of frames from the original film, it can "freeze" action by reproducing a particular frame continuously, or it can run the original film backwards so that the new film details the original action in reverse. The printer is so versatile that it has been described as the "basic tool of trick photograpy."

Metropolis (1926) A mechanical fantasy.

The Big Bangs

Explosions, gunfire, crashing aircraft, and ordinary streets becoming battlefields are the stuff that most action and adventure movies are made of. The special effects crew's job on such films is to ensure that explosive scenes can be filmed realistically, with the maximum safety for the actors and stunt people involved.

Fiery explosions and battlefield simulations call for "powder effects." Among the explosive devices used for powder effects are thunderflashes – sealed cardboard tubes containing black powder or flash powder – which resemble blasts from cannon shells or high velocity rifles. Also used are ground maroons, which make bigger explosions and are basically large thunderflashes with heavy string or twine wound around them to increase the explosive effect.

Such devices make their own smoke, but if more is required, smoke pots – cans containing chemical mixtures that give off smoke when ignited – are used. Shrapnel effects are frequently nothing more than paper bags filled with bits of black cardboard and flash powder exploded by a time fuse. When they're thrown in the air and detonated, the black cardboard looks like lethal metal shards cutting through the air.

Battlefield explosions are usually carefully mapped, with actors choreographed for filming to avoid danger areas. But things can go wrong. In *The Longest Day* (1962) when the D-Day landings of WWII were re-enacted, so many smoke-giving explosions were going off that two actors lost their route and ran into the danger areas. They are seen in the film literally being blown into the air – but thankfully both escaped serious injury.

Shoot to Thrill

Things have come a long way since Jimmy Cagney had real bullets – yes, *real bullets* – fired at him in some of the 1930s gangster movies. These days the line of bullets that explode on a wall just behind a fleeing actor will probably be small plastic-covered detonators called bullet hits, which are triggered electronically. And when the actor is finally nailed by gunfire, he'll almost certainly be wearing bullet plates. There are several kinds of bullet plates, but they all have a metal plate and plenty of foam padding to protect the actor from the explosive effects. The bullet plate is concealed beneath the actor's clothes, which are authentically holed when the bullet hit detonates. A blood sac immediately behind the bullet hit will burst when it detonates to make a gunshot wound gruesomely realistic.

A truck explodes in the James Bond film "The Living Daylights", 1987.

Make Way for the Model

When a scene calls for ships or aircraft to be blown to pieces in films, models will almost always be used. One of the most recent and best examples of such model work is *Top Gun*, which featured a lot of actual jet fighter footage intercut with models for the explosive scenes. The models varied considerably in size, and some individual models had to be made of different materials. For example, one shot called for a wing to be blown off a plane while the rest of the plane remained intact. The parts to be left undamaged were made of highly resilient fiberglass, while the exploding wing section was made of lightweight fragmentable polyurethane resins. The whole plane was suspended from cable and the explosive in the wing was detonated by remote control. Several new wing sections were cast so that they could be fitted to the undamaged fuselage if more takes were needed, but the shot was perfect first time around.

The Big Beasts

Much effects work between the 30s and 50s concentrated upon bringing terrifying creatures to the screens. One reason for that is possibly the success achieved by the first real monster movie, *King Kong*.

Kong's creator was the technical director of the film, Willis O'Brien. In previous features like *The Lost World* and *Creation*, O'Brien had skillfully combined stop-motion model animation with scaled-down sets and rear-projected live action. In this technique, he projected film from behind onto a translucent screen positioned behind a new subject, so that the existing film and the new subject could be re-filmed together. When they saw footage from *Creation*, RKO executives were convinced that a thrilling story they had about a giant ape could be made, and *King Kong* went into production.

A Model Performance

The filmmakers did use some full-sized props, such as Kong's arm and hand, which is seen holding the film's heroine so often. The bulk of Kong's part, however, was played by several 18-inch-high models used for the stop-motion photography. Each had a metal frame with movable limbs, head, mouth, and eyes. The frame was covered with rubber and sponge and coated with rabbit fur. We can see how such a makeshift monster was made to look real if we take Kong's climb up the outside of the Empire State Building at the end of the film as an example.

The Empire State Building was a miniature version of the real building with tiny pegs fitted to one side. The model Kong was attached to the pegs and photographed in position to make one frame of film. The model was then moved fractionally and photographed again. As many as 12 frame exposures might be needed for Kong to make just one climbing step up the building. But when this was shown to audiences at the rate of 24 frames per second, they saw Kong scaling the Empire State by making two climbing steps every second.

Benefits For Youngsters

O'Brien refined his work still further in a later giant ape movie called *Mighty Joe Young*, for which he won a Special Effects Oscar. Working with him on the model animation for that movie was young Ray Harryhausen, who has gone on to film some of the film industry's most fantastic model animation scenes. These have included a dinosaur rampaging through Coney Island's amusement park in *The Beast from 20,000 Fathoms*, seven fearsome sword-fighting skeletons in *Jason and the Argonauts,* and Pegasus, a flying winged horse in *Clash of the Titans.* As with O'Brien's work, the hallmarks of Harryhausen's effects are the seamless ways in which he combines his model animation with the live action, giving his creations a chilling reality.

Not all movie monsters have been animated models, however. Some have been mechanical effects, and others have been human, more or less.

Monstrous Make-up

Before Willis O'Brien made *King Kong*, he wanted to film Frankenstein, using stop-motion and an animated model for the monster. In the 1931 version of *Frankenstein*, however, Boris Karloff played the monster, using a lot of make-up, of course. The false top to his head and his eyelids were rubber, there were steel braces on Karloff's legs to make his movements stiff, and on his feet were boots normally worn by asphalt layers. Shoe polish blackened his fingernails and blue-green grease paint, which photographs grey, was smeared over his face.

The next classic monster on the screen was *The Wolf Man*, portrayed by Lon Chaney, Jr. The full make-up involved a molded rubber nose, artificial fangs and masses of yak hair which virtually covered the actor's face and hands. For the famous transformation scene, pieces of make-up were carefully removed in 21 separate stages. Each stage was recorded on a few frames of film. It took 22 hours to film the whole sequence, which lasts roughly 10 seconds on the screen. This 10 seconds of film footage remains a fine example of how effects, stop-motion filming, and make-up can work together.

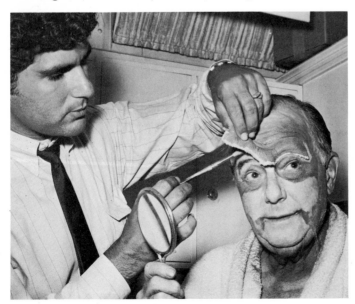

More Monkey Business

Movie make-up is film illusion at its simplest: making reality for film audiences by altering the natural appearance of actors. This can be either incidental, by adding a touch of color to a face to enhance character for the camera, or it can be fundamental, by sculpting an entire new look for an actor playing a fantasy creature. One of the finest examples of such fundamental change has been the simian make-up designed by John Chambers for *Planet of the Apes* and its sequels.

Chambers faced the problem of creating make-up that would keep the individuality of each actor and still give an overall ape appearance. The problem was further complicated because the actors would be in make-up for long periods, so the materials used had to be "wearer-friendly."

Chambers began by drawing ape characteristics on photographs of the principle actors, allowing the ape features to dominate without obliterating their basic human personalities. Casts or molds of the actors' faces were taken and clay was used to sculpt ape features onto these human molds. When the desired ape/human face was ready, a mold of that was made. Chambers had come up with a latex material, like foam rubber, that looked like ape skin but allowed the wearer to perspire through the material rather than under it. This latex was poured into the ape/human face molds to create the final masks worn for filming.

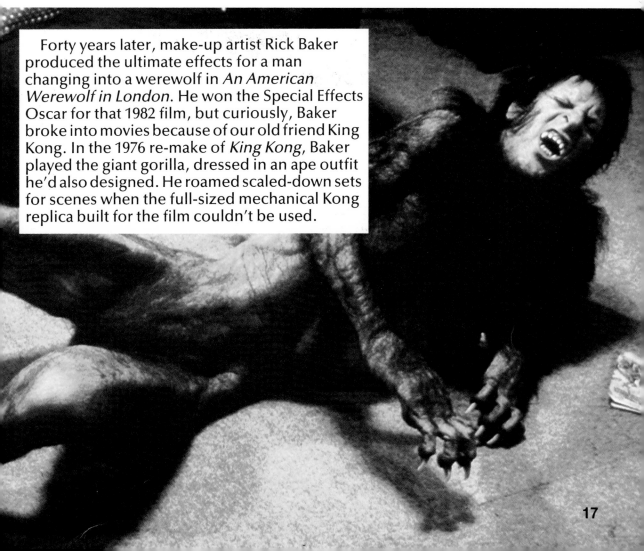

Forty years later, make-up artist Rick Baker produced the ultimate effects for a man changing into a werewolf in *An American Werewolf in London*. He won the Special Effects Oscar for that 1982 film, but curiously, Baker broke into movies because of our old friend King Kong. In the 1976 re-make of *King Kong*, Baker played the giant gorilla, dressed in an ape outfit he'd also designed. He roamed scaled-down sets for scenes when the full-sized mechanical Kong replica built for the film couldn't be used.

Special Effects in the Late Sixties

You can tell that *Planet of the Apes* was a commercial success by the number of sequels – four in all – that followed it. The first Apes film was released in 1968, the same year as another movie containing superior special effects: *2001: A Space Odyssey.* These two films demonstrated advances in effects technology that provided greater realism in science fiction films. *2001* contained the first examples of front projection effects and employed some traditional effects techniques in original and innovative ways.

Front Projection

In front projection, a background setting is projected on a screen behind the actors from a light source that is in front of those actors. The projector is placed at a 90-degree angle to the camera. Between the projector and the camera is a half-silvered mirror which both reflects light and allows light to pass through it. The mirror reflects the projected background setting past the actors onto the screen behind them.

Careful lighting on the set will wash out any of the projected image that might appear on the front of the actors. Shadows cast on the screen aren't detected by the camera as long as it views the projected image along the same axis as its light source. The screen used needs to be highly reflective so that it can send the projected image back through the mirror into the camera, which records the actors and the projected background together.

An Odyssey of Effects

An odyssey is a long trip full of adventure, and in *2001* the trip to Jupiter in the spaceship *Discovery* was certainly that. In the story, the ship is 700 feet long, though in reality two models were used. One was 54 feet long and one, used for distance views, was just 15 feet long.

One close shot in the film was particularly interesting. The longer model was moved slowly along a length of track by the effects crew. On its first trip, it was filmed with all the windows blacked out, which "saved" those blacked-out areas of film for later use as Méliès had done years before. The film was rewound and the model returned for a second trip. This time the entire ship was blacked out and white cards were positioned over the ship's windows. These white cards acted as miniature projection screens onto which previously filmed scenes of the astronauts at work were front-projected. The model's second trip along the track proceeded at exactly the same pace as the first. The camera automatically combined film of activity inside the ship with film of its exterior.

In addition to the excellent spacecraft scenes in the film – including scenes of a space station and a docking craft whirling through space while Strauss's Blue Danube Waltz is heard on the sound track – *2001* climaxes when an astronaut arrives at Jupiter and is plunged through a time warp. This was represented by a dazzling display of light effects created by Douglas Trumbull detailing an infinite corridor of light and shapes seemingly bombarding the camera at tremendous speed. In reality, it was the camera that moved slowly towards the light effects. It took one minute to travel towards them, but during that time just one frame of film was exposed. When the many frames exposed that way are projected together, audiences are unable to detect they are watching a highly elaborate stop-motion effect.

The Star Wars Trilogy

It was almost ten years after the release of *2001* that the science fiction movie made its giant leap forward. Despite the high quality of the effects in *2001*, the film itself was not a great commercial success. It took almost five years to earn enough to cover its production costs. Any film that could combine a "mass appeal" story with exceptional special effects work would clearly be successful. *Star Wars* was just such a film.

Star Wars, as conceived by producer George Lucas, needed special effects work that had never been done before. Many of the scenes Lucas envisaged meant designing and constructing an entirely new camera system. Partly for this reason, Lucas set up his own special effects company called Industrial Light & Magic. John Dykstra was the man at the head of the company. It was Dykstra, along with Douglas Trumbull, who devised the new Motion Control Camera System needed to bring the battling spacecraft to the screen.

Motion Control At Work

In the past, to combine two elements from two separate pieces of film and make one whole image on a new piece of film, you had to photograph each element with a camera fixed in one position. The new camera system made movement of the camera position possible and gave far greater realism to the effect.

For example, suppose you wanted to show people in the foreground running away from a giant ball of fire behind them.

Before the invention of the Motion Control System, you would black out the area above the people – the area where the ball of fire will appear – when you filmed the people. Then you film the ball of fire itself. When both elements are re-filmed together, the ball of fire fills in the blacked-out area above the people, and you have the footage you need.

But the new Motion Control System has a computer memory. It allows you to pan your camera across the scene, making it more realistic. You would film your people with the area blacked out above them as before, but move the camera at the speed and angle you desired. The computer in the system remembers that precise speed and angle and will duplicate the camera movement exactly when you film the ball of fire. The two elements therefore dovetail perfectly on every single frame of film when both elements are re-filmed together.

Of course, the computer can reproduce the same speed and angle of camera movement time and time again. That means it is possible to film and later combine as many elements as you wish to make your final image, so that whole fleets of spacecraft can be seen to battle and interact. You can, in other words, make a film like *Star Wars*!

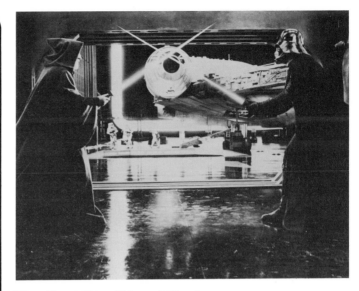

The Best Star Wars Effect

The Motion Control Camera System worked well for *Star Wars*, and as the system was revised and improved, its full potential became apparent in the films that followed: *The Empire Strikes Back* and *Return of the Jedi*. In those movies, more varied and complicated camera movements were made, involving greater numbers of elements to be added together. Even realistic speed blurring was being added to vehicles by the computer. But of all the fantastic effects we've seen in the Star Wars trilogy, perhaps the most important remains the very first one we saw at the opening of *Star Wars*. Had that not worked so well, had that not grabbed our attention and convinced us that we were watching space ships travel across the void, we may never have returned for more.

The shot was achieved using a model that was just over three feet long. Originally, it was thought that a model 50 feet in length would be needed, but time and money were tight. Richard Edlund, who was the photographic effects designer on the Star Wars films, did a test for the opening shot on a model that was less than two inches long, unceremoniously held in position on some wire. The test looked so good that it was clear the effect could be achieved with a much smaller model. It was photographed to make us think that a huge, rumbling spacecraft was sliding over our heads in deep space – and it worked perfectly.

Model Work in the Star Wars Films

The invention of the Motion Control Camera System was crucial to the making of *Star Wars*, but equally vital was the use of models to portray spacecraft and other vehicles or equipment.

Models vary in size according to the nature of the shot required. The models for the Walkers seen at the beginning of *The Empire Strikes Back* were built in different sizes. They ranged from two inches tall, for Walkers seen in distance shots, to 15 inches tall for the stop-motion filming, and up to four feet tall for one model used in the scene were a Walker crashes to the ground.

Some shots require models to be constructed so they add depth, or perspective, to a particular scene. A model may taper off quite dramatically towards the rear, while the front section is made quite wide. Such "forcing of perspective" when viewed from head-on makes the model seem much longer than it is. By the time it is seen on the screen, viewers think they see a spacecraft which might well be several miles long.

Stop-Motion Model Work

Stop-motion animation of models is a long, slow process which has been available to special effects designers for decades. We've already seen some of its applications in earlier chapters, and for the Empire Walkers, the techniques used were very similar. The model was photographed to make one frame of film. It was then moved fractionally and photographed again to make the next frame. These steps were repeated until the sequence was complete. What was unique about the Star Wars films and their stop-motion work was that their model animation could be combined with so many other elements using the Motion Control Camera System to give the scenes much more authenticity. Indeed, the special effects teams working on those films came to aptly refer to the process as go-motion!

Models and the Motion Control System

In the previous chapter, we saw that it is necessary to isolate elements of the action on film so that those elements can later be added with others to create the final image. With models, this is a fairly simple process. Suppose we want a model to fly across space while our camera shifts position as it records this. The model would first be filmed against an entirely blue screen background. This neutral background can then be processed out of the model film, leaving the model moving along on a clear field. Next, the blue-screen shot is printed onto black and white film, giving us a protection mask that will preserve the exact flight path of the model when we come to film the space background. When we film the background of a star-studded space, the system's computer memory ensures that the camera movement is repeated precisely, and the mask ensures that the model flight path on the second film remains unexposed. The two pieces of film are then re-filmed together, and the outcome is a spacecraft hurtling across a starry horizon.

23

More Star Wars Secrets: The Matte Artist

The full cost of making *Star Wars*, though high, would have been astronomical if all the film's sets had been fully constructed. The film crew would have had to have worked in outer space themselves much of the time if every scene you saw was entirely real. To keep costs down and at the same time create realistic settings for action, film producers call on the services of a matte artist to produce painted settings.

A matte shot is a composite image of live action and painting which has been painstakingly rendered to match the live action in every detail. The methods used to combine the matte painting with live action vary according to the problems to be overcome, but two methods are most common. Often a painting is made ahead of time and filmed when the live action itself is filmed – by having the painting on glass which is positioned in front of the camera. Sometimes the painting is made after the live action has been filmed. The artist rear-projects the already filmed live action onto glass, paints in the new detail necessary around the filmed scene, and then re-photographs the glass painting and the filmed scene together, creating a new image which will be seen in the final film.

For example, in one *Star Wars* scene, Ben Kenobi walks across a narrow ledge over the immensely deep power shaft of the Deathstar. In reality, the ledge was only three feet above the floor in the studio where the scene was shot. All that yawning depth was added later by a matte artist, Harrison Ellenshaw. The live-action element of the scene was filmed and later back-projected onto glass. Ellenshaw then painted around this "window" of live action, mostly beneath it to add all that depth. These two elements were then filmed as they appeared together, to give the final thrilling image we saw on the screen.

Mattes to the Rescue

As well as adding considerably to a set, or incorporating buildings or elements to scenes that would be impossible to construct, matte artists are also called upon to rescue film that has already been shot but contains a mistake. Any historical movie, for example, might call for exterior locations with nearby modern buildings that mistakenly appear in the scene when it is filmed. In such circumstances, a matte artist would paint out the offending buildings.

The Glass Shot Matte Method

Suppose you wished to film a scene of a man standing on one side of the screen looking up at a huge space ship that has just landed on Earth. To build a spaceship that size would be incredibly expensive. But the scene could be filmed by having the space ship painted onto a section of glass and leaving the rest of the glass clear. The glass is then positioned in front of the camera and lined up with the real landscape. The live action can now be filmed through the glass. The result is that the man, seen through the clear portion of the glass, apparently stares up at a huge space ship.

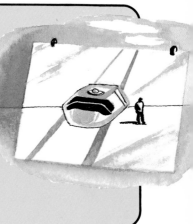

Fantastic though the work of the matte artist is, we should not be able to detect that parts of a scene have been painted and aren't real. As Harrison Ellenshaw himself says, "As much as I would like people to notice my work, ironically, I'm only successful if they can't!"

Still More Star Wars Secrets: Mechanical Effects

Mechanical Facts to Chew Over

The mechanical effect is designed to look real, and not mechanical at all. One of the most famous mechanical effects was so "real," though, it even earned an affectionate name from the effects crew operating it. This was Bruce, 25 feet of mechanical great white shark, who took the title role in *Jaws*.

In all, three mechanical sharks were built to portray the shark. Two were on platforms that ran along an underwater track. Each was one-sided and played the shark's left profile or its right. The third machine, Bruce, was complete and cost $150,000 to make. He was guided under the water by scuba divers, who also worked his tail and fins. His all-important jaws, however, worked by hydraulics. They were seen looking gruesomely realistic near the end of the film, when the great white shark appears to lunch on the shark hunter. Thankfully, the stuntman who appeared to be eaten alive later emerged from the mechanical mouth unharmed.

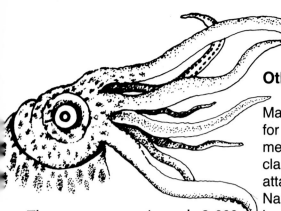

Other Mechanical Greats

Making the mechanical look real can be tricky even for an expert like Bob Mattey. He designed the mechanical sharks for *Jaws* and also created another classic monster of the deep – the giant squid that attacks Captain Nemo and his submarine the Nautilus in *20,000 Leagues Under the Sea*. The squid had tentacles connected to an air pump; when air was sucked out, the tentacles curled up, and when air was pumped in, they straightened. Movement of these lengthy tentacles was achieved by wires, but when the scene was first shot – with a calm sea and red sunset background – the wires occasionally became visible, and the squid looked anything but real. The problem was solved by "obscuring the action" – filming the squid's attack as if it were taking place during a violent storm. The driving rain, crashing waves, and windswept sea spray added enormously to the drama of the scene and the realism of the squid.

There are approximately 2,000 separate special effects in the three Star Wars films. Some of these are termed mechanical effects – machines, usually constructed to play creatures that don't exist. They move by various means, such as pulleys, compressed air, or hydraulics. Luke Skywalker is seen riding the Tauntaun across the frozen planet of Hoth at the beginning of *The Empire Strikes Back*. In close-ups, we're actually seeing actor Mark Hamill sitting on an eight feet tall, fur-covered machine which can rear up, blink, and even blow carbon dioxide out of its nose.

Obscuring the action worked well with another fearsome mechanical monster in *Alien*, designed by H. R. Giger, with Carlo Rambaldi creating the head mechanics. This time, though, the trick was used to add tension, because the design of the creature was so convincing that when it was finally seen, at the end of *Alien* and in the sequel, *Aliens*, the creature looked frighteningly real!

Carlo Rambaldi also created another mechanical character – the most popular mechanical so far created for the movies. This time it wasn't a monster, but E.T., for the movie *E.T.: the Extra-Terrestrial*.

Industrial Light & Magic:
Special Effects Wizards

In 1975, George Lucas was ready to begin shooting the special effects for *Star Wars*. But rather than hand over the effects work to an independent company, Lucas decided to set up his own facility. He called it Industrial Light & Magic Incorporated, putting John Dykstra in charge.

It had humble beginnings, with an empty warehouse base in the San Fernando Valley in Southern California. Equipment, apart from one table and a telephone, was non-existent. But Dykstra recruited some 70 young effects people and turned the empty warehouse into a functional studio. Traditional working practices went by the board; people dressed as they liked and worked without set hours. The studio doors were open 24 hours a day. And although each member of the crew brought his or her own special skill to ILM, they continually tried working in different areas of effects production. A year and a half later, the crew went their separate ways, their work completed. Although they were pleased with their efforts, they had no idea that the film would prove so successful.

When Lucas decided to move the operation to San Rafael in northern California to work on *The Empire Strikes Back*, rehiring most of the original crew was easy. Dykstra, however, stayed at the old ILM warehouse to form his own effects company, Apogee. But ILM has continued to set the standards in the special effects world. Besides the three Star Wars films, it has produced effects for both the *Indiana Jones* movies, the last three *Star Trek* films, *E.T.*, *Back to the Future*, *Cocoon*, and many others. Of the 10 most successful films of all time, half of them boast effects produced by ILM.

An Arkful of Ideas

Trying to single out an effect to typify Industrial Light & Magic is difficult, but the climactic scenes of *Raiders of the Lost Ark* give some idea of both the ingenuity and flexibility within ILM. Model maker Steve Gawley had built a miniature set for the scenes when the Nazis open up the Ark, bringing upon themselves the wrath of God. A terrible fire storm rages above them, sucking the soldiers up from the ground. Cleverly, Gawley built his set upside down. This meant that when the film of the scene was reversed, the movement of the seven inch tall model soldiers and the flames from the fire storm looked much more realistic.

The same scenes, though, called for a number of ghosts to be released from the Ark. Several ideas had been tried to achieve these effects, but none had worked. Then model maker Gawley suggested that film of ghost-shaped pieces of silk trailed and swished through water via thin sticks might work. The effect was filmed through the glass sides of a water tank, and later combined with the rest of the live action. Naturally enough, it was Gawley who got the job of "animating" the ghost silks through the water.

Special Effects Animation

Just as matte artists consider they've been successful when an audience can't detect their work, the same is true for animation artists when they add effects to live action film. They want the audience to believe in the effect they are seeing without realizing that it is animation. Much animation today occurs in science fiction films where laser weaponry or rocket ship engines need to blast or burn. We're about to discover that all this futuristic technology is usually powered by an animator's pencil.

Animation Masters

Disney productions, naturally enough, are renowned for the high quality of their animation effects. The company has a permanent animation unit, which was kept very busy on *The Black Hole*, a space adventure movie featuring more than 350 animated effects scenes. Laser battles between humans and robots abounded, and mighty spacecraft blasted across the galaxy. In reality, some quite down-to-earth procedures were used to make such scenes work.

Each single frame of film that required animation was photocopied, and the copy later positioned on an animator's table. White drawing paper was placed over the photocopy and pinned to stay in register while the strong light in the animator's table enabled the photocopied image to be seen through the paper. The animation artist then drew the effect required for that frame of film onto the paper, using black pencil only. The completed pencil drawing was photographed in black and white to create an optical matte for the effect. These mattes were then combined with the actual live footage when the film was "copied" in the optical printer. The printer could add whatever color was necessary for the effect. Relaxing or tightening the focusing on the matte gave either soft-edged or sharp-edged color effects. For example, in the film the laser weapon blasts have sharp, white-hot cores, with softer defused coloring on either side. These blasts are a fiery testament to the power of the artist's pencil.

A Finishing Touch

In addition to forming the basis of an effect, animation can be added to other effects to improve the illusion. In Hitchcock's *The Birds*, for example, some hand-drawn birds were added to the footage of real and mechanical ones to swell the number of winged attackers. Explosion scenes in many films often have effects animation added to enhance the look and power of the blasts. And the laser swords used by Ben Kenobi and Darth Vader for their duel in *Star Wars* needed something extra to go with the front projection effects employed to produce the laser light in the live action footage. That "something extra" was provided by animated light effects.

Storyboarding An Effect

When a new film script arrives on the desk of a special effects designer, there's always the possibility that it will contain every designers' favorite phrase: "with an effect unlike anything seen before!" To meet such a challenge designers must rely more than usual on the planning method adopted before every effect is undertaken. This method is known as storyboarding.

Storyboarding an effect means making numerous sketches and drawings of all the component parts that will be necessary for a particular effect to work. Breaking the effect down in this manner enables the designer to know how he will come to film a scene, shot by shot. He will know what needs to be built, what can be filmed with models, what will require animation, and what will prove just too costly to film.

Last Starfighter.

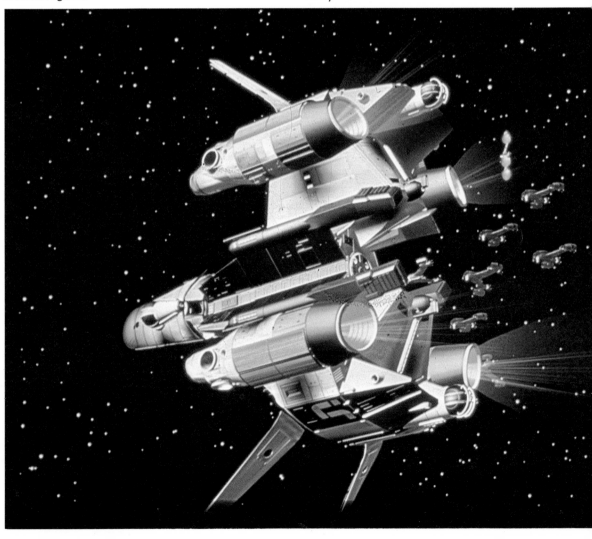

1. Attacking spacecraft.
2. Lazer weaponry (animated effects).
3. Damaged spacecraft.

4. Damage
5. Matte painting of background starfield.

A Typical Piece of Storyboarding

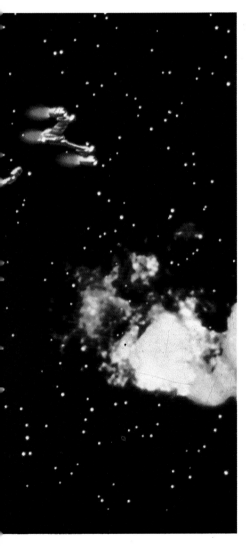

Suppose we are asked to film a scene from a space adventure in which two spacecrafts pursue each other across a starry horizon. One spaceship is firing laser weapons at the other, and has hit its target several times already. A final laser blast destroys the second craft. Let's concentrate on the split-second in the scene when the pursuing craft is firing that final laser charge at its victim.

Careful storyboarding will show that at this point in the scene, five different effects are required, each of which needs to be produced separately. Later all five will be combined to put this split-second of action on the screen.

The first effect is the attacking spacecraft. This would be a model filmed using a motion control camera system. Second, we need the laser weaponry, which would be provided by animated effects work. Next, we must show the damaged spacecraft by filming a different model with the motion control camera. Fourth, the damage to this craft will necessitate further animation. Finally, there is the star field behind both spacecraft, which could be provided by a matte painting.

Each of these five effects requires its own piece of negative film. And only when all five pieces are put together is a sixth piece of film – of the scene as it would appear in the theater – made. To forget even one of these effects elements, of course, would completely ruin the scene. Effects designers cannot allow that to happen, and accurate storyboarding makes sure that it doesn't.

Classic Effects I: How Superman Flew

Is it a bird? Is it a plane? No, it's actor Christopher Reeve suspended on wires, variously combined with backgrounds and sometimes model cityscapes. One such method of combination was the Zoptic System developed by Zoran Perisic – a classic effect which really does make you think a man can fly.

Superman's Cape

Superman was seen to fly when in fact he never moved an inch. A problem, though, was that if his cape wasn't moving when Superman was appearing to fly, no one would be convinced by the illusion.

The Zoptic System

To begin with, the effect requires the background setting for the flight to be filmed. This film is then projected onto an angled two-way mirror, which reflects the filmed background onto a screen. Superman is then suspended in front of this screen on carefully concealed wires (if necessary, they can be matte-painted out later). The film camera shoots the footage we see in the theater through the viewing side of the two-way mirror, recording the projected background and the "live" Superman together.

So far so good. But realistic movement must be added to the flight. The filming camera and the projector are both fitted with zoom lenses which are synchronized. As the projector lens alters focal length, the background diminishes. Simultaneously, the filming camera lens zooms in to compensate, so that the diminished background appears to stay the same size in the camera. But having zoomed in, the camera records the Superman figure appearing to get larger. Because he seems to be getting larger against a background that seems unchanged, the effect is of Superman flying towards the audience.

Wind machines were tried at first, but the results weren't convincing. In the end, a radio-controlled system using fishing tackle-type rods with lines attached to the cape was invented. The system rippled and flapped the cape exactly on cue.

A Super Idea

Alexander and Ilya Salkind spent five years planning *Superman: The Movie*. Much of that time was dedicated to devising the manner in which Superman would be seen to fly. The special effect they originaly hoped for to open the movie, however, would certainly have been the most spectacular ever attempted. The idea was to project film of Superman flying in the movie theater itself. He would appear over the heads of the audience, before he flew to the screen, whereupon the film, in the conventional sense, would begin. This ambitious effect proved impossible to achieve at the time. Given the tremendous advances made in special effects work over the years, it or something similar may yet happen.

Classic Effects II:
The USS Enterprise

The Enterprise, call sign NCC-1701, has always been more than just a mode of transport for Captain Kirk and his crew. The starship, able to support a self-contained community in deep space, is one of the main characters in the Star Trek series. Since it was first seen on NBC TV back in 1966, the ship has been through a lot. When it made its debut in the cinema, the original, small-screen *Enterprise* was modified, though the basic shape remained the same. In the second Star Trek movie it suffered considerable battle damage, and in the third it was destroyed. Happily, in *Star Trek IV – The Voyage Home*, a "new" *Enterprise* is seen with Kirk once more at the helm. Originally conceived as a vessel 947 feet long, 417 feet wide, and weighing 190,000 tons, this "new" Enterprise is in fact just 8 feet long and made of tough, lightweight plastics. It is, of course, a model – the same one which has been seen in all four Star Trek movies to date.

Even Models Need Make-Up

The damage sustained to the Enterprise in the second and third films was created by adding materials to the model, in much the same way an actor would acquire blood and bruise make-up after a fight scene. Laser hits to the hull were inflicted by adding rubber cement to the affected areas. This was then painted black with an airbrush to give the charred effects. Pieces of foil were attached to resemble shards of metal peeling away from the damaged structure. For the "new" *Enterprise*, all this make-up was removed, and the model was repainted. In a thoughtful touch, the *Enterprise* call sign on the main saucer was amended to read NCC-1701-A.

All In A Day's Warp

At the end of *Star Trek IV*, the *Enterprise* does what a starship does best, and accelerates away from us at warp speed. The ship's maximum speed is warp seven. (Warp one is the speed of light.) The visual effect for the *Enterprise* going to warp speed has always been to have the model dissolve into colored light streaks. The smooth and impressive warp effect in *Star Trek IV*, though, was achieved in three stages, because the aim was to show the ship making a long zoom away from the camera.

The first stage involved motion-controlled model photography matched with optical animated effects, adjusted frame by frame to maintain the correct point of origin as the ship moved away. The second stage was to switch the model for a transparency of the ship and move that away from the camera to lengthen the *Enterprise*'s zoom – again matching it with light animation, which once more had to be altered frame by frame. Finally, the transparency was faded out, leaving just the animated effects on the screen – and a satisfied audience thrilling at yet another superb *Enterprise* warp!

Special Effects For Fun

The tradition among special effects creators is to refer to their work as "gags," and indeed effects are often used to create laughter in the theater. Producing humorous effects, however, is a serious business; funny scenes are often the most dangerous for those performing them, and their safety is essential.

For example, actors and stuntmen are frequently asked to fly and hurtle through the air to entertain us. Controlling their flight to keep them safe usually involves flying them on wires. A hip harness is fitted with a wire at each hip, suspending the wearer from a transportable rig. The wires need to be thin, so they can't be detected on screen, and strong, to support the actor or stuntman. Without a doubt, the finest examples of wire work flying sequences to date can be seen in the Superman movies.

Wire work can also help non-humans, such as the Muppets. Kermit, Miss Piggy, and the rest are hand puppets, but some scenes, such as when Kermit rode a bike in *The Muppet Movie*, need to be "look – no hands" puppetry to work. Kermit went for his ride with the help of wires and nearly invisible single-fiber threads, disguised by careful lighting and camera angles.

Filming human characters to appear alongside cartoon characters is another area of comedy which naturally calls for serious special effects work. Usually the live action is filmed first. Then a silhouette matte image is created that matches it frame for frame. This is combined with hand-drawn animation film, again with a corresponding frame-for-frame matte image, onto a separately filmed live or animated background scene.

An optical printer is used, and when the background film is passed through, the two sets of mattes "save" areas on the new copy of the background film. But since these two saved areas match both the live and animated film frame for frame, both sequences slot seamlessly onto the new background, where they appear to interact together. This process worked superbly in *Mary Poppins*, particularly when the human characters appear to dance with a group of animated penguins.

The recent and enormously popular *Ghostbusters*, using computer-assisted animation camera systems, also blended live action with animated characters. Among the ghost characters that needed busting was Onionhead, the greedy green ghoul who haunted a hotel and always tried to eat the guests' dinners. Any food or drink he swallowed, though, always fell straight through him onto the floor or table. Onionhead was an animated effect that had to stay ghostly transparent even when matched with solid objects like plates of food or a bottle of wine. The "wine" from the bottle, seen flowing right through Onionhead to stain a tablecloth beneath him, was an animated effect drawn frame by frame, although the stain was filmed "live" by having liquid pumped upwards from beneath the tablecloth.

Trying to keep a check on these effect creations were the ghostbusting trio themselves, using their Nutrona Wand weapons. These fired what the effects designers described as a "rubberized laser." It was created by layer upon layer of effects artwork backed up with real light effects, which helped to match the artwork to the live action more convincingly. Audiences everywhere loved it, even if the ghosts didn't.

Video Effects to Try Yourself

If you have access to a video camera and recorder either at home or at school, it's possible to try some simple visual effects. Because video is a different medium than film, not all the "areas of intervention" mentioned in the first chapter are available to video users with basic equipment, but some forms of illusion can still be achieved.

First, you can alter what the camera records by applying optical devices to the lens. The simplest method is to fix a shaped mask – perhaps a star cut-out on card – to the lens, so that the sequence is seen inside the star. If available, shoot through star filters or prismatic lenses for interesting light effects or multiple images. Or an ordinary glass filter can be lightly smeared with grease to give a scene a misty effect. Also, shooting through large panes of rippled glass will give unusual picture distortions.

Glass and Mirror Tricks

Besides picture distortions, glass can also help when captions need to be added. Using felt pen, you can write on clear glass and position this about 18 inches from the camera. Focusing on the caption will blur all the background, but start to refocus on the background and the caption will eventually disappear. The trick also works in reverse.

Mirrors are commonly used in special effects and they can assist video users too. The easiest trick is a wipe effect, where a second picture appears to replace the first by pushing it to one side and off the screen. Set the camera up to record the second image, then place a mirror between the camera and the image at a 45 degree angle to the camera. Now set up the first image to one side of the camera, so that it appears in the mirror. Be sure that the first image is the same distance from the mirror as the second, and begin recording the first image reflection in the mirror. When you pull away the mirror, you will achieve a wipe from the first image to the second. Variations using different mirror angles or more mirrors are virtually endless.

Animation and Stop-Motion

Some limited tricks are possible using a video camera with a pause button, as long as you can keep camera and background completely steady by fixing the camera rigidly to a tripod. Unusual, jerky animation of lifeless objects is possible by recording, pausing, moving the object slightly, recording, pausing, and so on. Choose the subject of your animation carefully, so that the illusion is helped by the harsh animation.

You can also repeat one of Méliès's early tricks in making objects disappear. With the camera rigid and a constant background, you can record someone holding a book, for example. Press pause, keep your actor "frozen" while you quickly remove the book, and then begin recording the actor looking baffled because his book is missing. Pause again, quickly supply your frozen actor with a different book, and begin recording his surprised reactions once more.

All these illusions take time to perfect, but the advantage of video is that you can instantly play back your recording. If the trick hasn't worked, simply rewind and begin again. This may happen frequently at first, but patience and practice will improve your results. Eventually, you'll have some perfect illusions – and renewed admiration, no doubt, for the professionalism of those who create effects for a living.

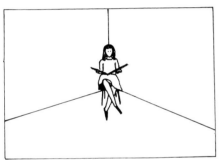

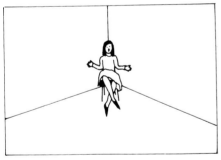

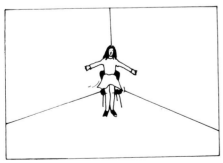

Effects In The Future

Computer-controlled camera systems have helped effects designers enormously in recent years, allowing them to produce, among other things, stunningly realistic battle scenes in space. But the computer is already proving that it has much more to offer the special effects industry than merely controlling cameras.

The next giant leap forward is the computer-generated visual effects entirely composed by computer graphics.

A Glimpse of Things to Come

Two films to date have made significant use of such computer effects. In *Tron*, the hero journeys inside a computer and ends up playing its video games for real. Nearly 14 minutes of pure computer graphics were seen in the film. One of the computer images produced for the movie was the Light Cycle, a futuristic motorbike from one of the video games. The Light Cycle began life as an artist's drawing. From this, details of its dimensions, coloring and so on were programmed into the effects computer so that it could generate a solid image of the Light Cycle on screen. Under instruction, the computer could further show its created image making any movements required, from any requested angle.

The Last Starfighter contained more than 30 minutes of computer generated effects created by two programmers, John Whitney and Gary Demos. They used a Cray XMP computer, a powerful machine capable of performing a mind-numbing several million operations per second. It has the ability to simulate dog-fight battles between spacecraft, which is what it was mostly used for in the movie. Essentially, the computer scenes were on a par with motion-control model effects work, but were achieved without models, blue screens, animated laser effects, and everything else. Whitney and Demos believe they are just scratching the surface of what can be accomplished with computer graphics. Advances in computer technology are happening almost daily, and it's clear that a whole new era of special effects work is about to begin.

Whitney and Demos point out that there are some things they cannot yet simulate on computer. For example, they cannot create the subtleties of expression on human faces. That's how it should be – technology should, after all, serve us, not replace us. Computer graphic effects are at their best when used for subjects which audiences have no experience with, such as the insides of a computer or the depths of outer space. We can expect to see more computer graphics in films dealing with such subjects, and that's how it should be, too. This book began with the statement that special effects are used when film of dangerous, expensive, or impossible scenes is needed. The advent of computer graphics has turned much of the impossible into the possible.

Glossary

Animation   Character(s) represented by many different hand drawings. When filmed together using stop-motion techniques, these drawings appear to move.

Animation Effects   Hand-drawn or computer drawn additions to existing frames of film.

Back Projection   Film or slides projected onto a translucent screen from behind the screen to provide background scenes.

Blue Screen Shot   Method of inserting background into a picture. The subject is filmed against a blue screen and is isolated when the blue backing is filtered out. This process allows the subject to be combined with a separately recorded background.

Bullet Hit   Electrically fired plastic-coated detonator used to simulate a bullet hitting a target.

Cel   Transparent plastic sheet on which an animation artist completes his drawing or effect.

Composite Photography   Final filmed image when two or more separate pieces of film are combined together.

Dissolve   The technique of fading out one scene while fading in another.

Dump Tank   Large-volume water tank used for shots requiring water surges.

Frame   Single picture on strip of celluloid film. The normal rate of projection is 24 frames per second.

Freeze Frame   Continual projection of single frame of film, best achieved by having the frame repeated over and over on the strip of film.

Front Projection   Also called Front Axial Projection. The background scene is projected onto a highly reflective screen. Projection, through a half-silvered mirror, is on the same axis as the camera.

Glass Shot   Painting on glass positioned between camera and actor so that camera records painted image and live action together.

Half-Silvered Mirror   Partially silvered mirror which both reflects light and allows light to pass through it.

Maroons   Large explosive fireworks used to simulate shellfire.

Matte   See Optical Matte.

Matte Painting   Painting added to live action to form a composite scene.

Matte Shot   Final image when matte painting and live action are filmed together.

Mechanical Effects   Full-sized machines constructed to portray real or imagined creatures and vehicles.

Miniatures   Scaled down model buildings and/or scenery.

Model   Scaled down construction of vehicle or creature.

Motion Control Camera System   Method of recording (often via computer memory) camera movement, so that the camera can repeat the precise movement as many times as required. This allows for perfect compositing of many elements into one scene.

Optical Effects   Additions or amendments to scenes made in the laboratory at the film processing stage.

Optical Matte   Mask used to keep an area of film unexposed so that it can be used later.

Optical Printer   Device incorporating projector and camera to enable original film to be copied.

Powder Effects   Controlled explosions in live action scenes.

Rear Projection   See Back Projection.

Slow Motion   Projection at normal rate of frames per second of film recorded at more than the normal rate of frames per second. This slows down the filmed action.

Smoke Pots   Containers of chemicals that produce smoke when lit.

Speeded Motion   Projection at normal rate of frames per second of film recorded at less than the normal rate of frames per second. This speeds up the filmed action.

Stop-Motion Photography   Exposure of one frame of film at a time.

Storyboards   Sketches of sequence of shots, or elements within a particular shot, indicating what is required visually.

Stunts   Dangerous or difficult actions in a scene often undertaken by stunt artists standing in for the principal performers.

Thunderflashes   Explosive device used to simulate high velocity gunfire or cannon shells.

Visual Effects   Full-sized construction (in part or complete) of building, structure, vehicle or creature, built for filming.

Wipe   Removal of one picture by line tracking across it to reveal a second picture.

Wire Work   Suspending performers or objects on carefully concealed wires so that they appear to defy gravity.

Zoptic System   Camera system incorporating projector and camera fitted with synchronized zoom lenses. This system enables a projected background scene to remain constant while the camera zooms into a foreground subject. The result is that the foreground subject appears to move dramatically towards the camera.

Index

Acknowledgements

We would like to thank and acknowledge the following people for the use of their photo's and transparencies.

p. 6/7   Kobal Collection

p. 8/9   National Film Archive

p. 10/11   Kobal Collection

p.12/13   Topham Picture Library

p. 14/15   National Film Archive
           Kobal Collection

p. 16/17   Ronald Grant
           Kobal Collection

p. 18/19   Kobal Collection
           Ronald Grant

p. 20/21   Topham Picture Library
           National Film Archive

p. 22/23   Kobal Collection

p. 24/25   Ronald Grant
p. 26/27   National Film Archive

p. 28/29   Lucasfllm Ltd.

p. 30/31   Ronald Grant
           Topham Picture Library

p. 32/33   Ronald Grant

p. 34/35   Kobal Collection

p. 36/37   Kobal Colletion

p. 38/39   Topham Picture Library
           Kobal Collection

p. 40/41   Kobal Collection

Cover photo's
    Kobal Collection
    National Film Archive, London
    Artwork by Sharon Perks

Frontispiece:
    Ronald Grant
    Special Effects Crew

Design/Production: Susie Home
Text by: Ian Rimmer
Illustrations by: Sharon Perks